Felix
MENDELSSOHN

SAINT PAUL

An Oratorio

for Soli, Chorus and Orchestra
with German and English text

CHORAL SCORE

K 06298

INHALT.

PAULUS.

Erster Theil.

N.º 1. OUVERTURE.

Andante. (M.M. ♩=84.)

(Choral: „Wachet auf, ruft uns die Stimme.")

Bearbeitung von Aug. Horn.

11

12

Nº 2. CHOR.

Allegro maestoso.

19

20

Nᵒ 3. CHORAL.

№ 4. RECITATIV.

24

30

32

№ 6. RECITATIV.

Sopran Solo.

Und sie sa_hen auf ihn Al _ _ le, die im Ra_the sassen, und sa_hen sein
And all that sat in the Council look_ed steadfastly on him, and saw his

An_gesicht wie ei_nes En_gels Angesicht. Da sprach der Ho_he_priester: Ist dem al_
face as it had been the face of an An _ gel. Then said the High - Priest: Are these things

34

TEN: SOLO.

so? Stephanus sprach: / Lieben Brüder und Vä-ter, hö - ret
so? And Stephen said: / *Men, brethren, and fathers, hearken to*

Andante sostenuto.

zu. Gott der Herr-lichkeit erschien un-sern Vä-tern, er-ret-te-te das
me: The God of Glo-ry ap-pear-ed un-to our fathers, de-liv-er-ed the

Volk aus al-ler Trübsal und gab ih-nen Heil. A-ber sie ver-nah - men es nicht. Er sandte
people out of their afflictions, and gave them favour. But they un-derstood it not. He sent

Andante.

Mosen in Ae-gyp-ten, da er ihr Lei-den sah und hö-re-te ihr Seufzen.
Moses in-to E-gypt, for He saw their afflictions, and heard their groaning.

A-ber sie ver-leug-ne-ten ihn und wollten ihm nicht ge-hor-sam wer-den, und
But they re- -fu-sed him, and would not o-bey his word, but

+) Dies **Recit.** muss anfangs sehr ruhig, dann immer mehr *crescendo* und vom **Allegro molto** an mit voller Kraft vorgetragen werden.

wie eu_re Vä_ter, al_so auch ihr.
As did your fathers, ev'n so do ye!

Welche Pro_pheten ha_ben eu_re Vä_ter nicht ver_folgt?
Which of the Prophets have not your fa _ _ thers per_se_cuted?

die da zu_vor ver_kün_dig_ten die Zu_kunft
And they have slain them which showed be_fore the com _ _ ing

die _ ses Ge_rech _ ten, des_sen Mörder
of Him, the Just one, with whose murder

ihr ge_worden seid. Ihr habt das Ge_
ye have here been stain'd. Ye have receiv_ed the

38

N⁰ 7. ARIE.

Wie oft hab ich nicht deine Kin_der ver_sammeln
How oft_en would I have ga_thered unto M_thy

wol_len, und ihr habt nicht ge_wollt, und ihr habt nicht ge_wollt!
chil_dren, and ye would not, and ye would not!

Je_ru_sa_lem! Je_ru_sa_lem, die du töd_test die Pro-
Je_ru_sa_lem! Je_ru_sa_lem, thou that kill_est the

phe_ten, die du töd_test die zu dir gesandt.
Pro_phets, thou that ston_est them which are sent unto thee.

Je_ru_sa_lem! Je_ru_sa_lem!
Je_ru_sa_lem! Je_ru_sa_lem!

Nº 8. RECITATIV.

Tenor Solo.

Sie a_ber stürmten auf ihn ein, und stie_ssen ihn zur
Then they ran up_on him with one ac_cord, and cast him out of the

Stadt hin_aus, und stei_nig_ten ihn, und schrie_en laut:
ci _ _ ty and ston_ed him, and cried a _ loud:

Allegro moderato.

SOPRAN.

Stei _ niget ihn,
Stone him to death,

ALT.

Stei_ni_get ihn, stei _ niget ihn,
Stone him to death, stone him to death,

TENOR.

Stei_ni_get ihn, stei_ni_get ihn, stei _ niget ihn,
Stone him to death, stone him to death, stone him to death,

BASS.

Stei _ ni_get ihn, stei_ni_get ihn, stei _ _ _ _ niget ihn,
Stone him to death, stone him to death, stone_____ him to death,

Allegro moderato.

42

44

CHORAL.

48

N⁰ 10. RECITATIV.

Sopran Solo.

Und die Zeugen legten ab ih _ re Kleider zu den Füssen eines Jünglings, der hiess
And the witnesses had laid down their clothes at the feet of a young man whose name was

Saulus; der hat_te Wohlgefal_len an seinem To _ de. Es be_schickten a_ber Ste_phanum
Saul, who was consent_ing un_to his death. And de_vout men took Stephen, and

got_tes_fürch_ti_ge Männer, und hiel_ten ei_ne gro_sse Kla_ge ü_ber ihn.
car_ried him to his bu_rial, and made great la_men_ta_tion o_ver him.

N⁰ 11. CHOR.

Andante con moto.

cantabile

52

53

stirbt. doch wird die See _ _ le le _ ben.

dies, the soul shall live _ _ _ for ev _ er.

stirbt, doch wird die See _ _ le le _ ben.

dies, the soul shall live _ _ _ for ev _ er.

Nº 12. RECITATIV und ARIE.

stummen müs_sen sie! Ver_til_ge sie, Herr Ze_ba_
*let them feel Thy pow'r! Con_sume them all, Lord Sa_ba_*

oth, wie Stop_peln vor dem Feu_____er,
oth! Con_sume them all, con_sume Thine e_ne_mies!

lass dei_nen Zorn sie tref_fen, ver_stum_men müs_sen
Pour out Thine in_dig_na_tion, and let them feel Thy

sie, ver_stum_men müs___sen sie.____ Ver_
*pow'r, yea, let them feel Thy pow'r!____ Con_*

til_ge sie, Herr Ze_ba____oth, wie Stop_peln vor dem
sume them all, Lord Sa_ba____oth! Con_sume all these Thine

№ 13. RECITATIV und ARIOSO.

Sopran II.

Und zog mit ei_ner Schaar gen Da_mascus, und hat_te Macht und Be_
*And he journey'd with companions towards Da_mascus, and had autho_ri_ty and com_*

fehl von den Ho_hen_priestern, Män _ ner und Wei_ber ge_bun_den zu füh_ren
mand from the High - Priest, that he might bring them bound, men and wo_men,

gen Je_rusalem.
un_to Je_rusalem.

Arioso.
Andantino.

Doch der Herr ver_gisst der Seinen nicht, er ge_
*But the Lord is mindful of His own, He re_*

denkt seiner Kin _ der, doch der Herr vergisst der Seinen nicht, der
mem_bers His chil_ _ dren, but the Lord is mindful of His own, the

Herr ge_denkt seiner Kin_der, ge_denkt seiner Kin _ der.
Lord re_members His chil_dren, re_mem_ _ bers His chil_dren.

N⁰ 14. RECITATIV mit CHOR.

Nᵒ 15. CHOR.

Molto allegro con fuoco.

66

69

73

Nᵒ 16. CHORAL.

78

N°17. RECITATIV.

Nº 18. ARIE.

82

Tenor Solo.

Es war a_ber ein Jünger zu Da_mascus, mit Namen A_na_ni_as, zu
And there was a dis_ci_ple at Da_mascus, named A_na_ni_as; to

Andante. SOPRAN SOLO.

dem sprach der Herr: A_na_ni_as, ste_he auf! und
*him said the Lord: A_na_ni_as, a_rise! and en_*

fra_ge nach Saul von Tar_se, denn sie_he, er be_tet! die_ser ist mir ein
quire thou for Saul of Tar_sus, for behold, he pray_eth! He is a chos_en

aus_erwähltes Rüst_zeug; ich will ihm zei_gen, wie viel er
ves_sel un_to me, the Lord! and I will show un_to him how

Poco animato.

lei_den muss um meines Na_mens wil_len.
great things he must suf_fer for my Name's sake.

№ 20. ARIE mit CHOR.

Nº 21. RECITATIV.

Sopran Solo.

Und A_na_ni_as ging hin, und kam in das Haus, und leg_te die
And A_na_ni_us went his way, and enter'd in_to the house, and lay_ing his

TENOR SOLO.

Hän_de auf ihn und sprach: Lie_ber Bru_der Saul, der Herr hat mich gesandt, der dir er_
hands up_on him, said: "Hear thou, Bro_ther Saul! The Lord hath sent me hi_ther, ev_en

schie_nen ist auf dem We_ge, da du her_kamst, dass du wie_der
Je_sus that ap_peard un_to thee as thou ca_mest, that thou might'st re_ceive thy

se_hend und mit dem heil'gen Geist er_fül_let wer__dest.
sight, and be like_wise fill_ed with the Ho_ly Ghost!

Allegro molto.

N°22. CHOR.

98

*) Von hier muss das Tempo immer schneller werden bis Seite 100, Tact 5, Più animato.

Più animato.

A - men, A - men, A - men, A - men, sei

A - men, A - men, A - men, A - men, His

A - men, A - men, A - men, A - men, sei

A - men, A - men, A - men, A - men, His

Eh - - re in E - wig - keit, A - men, A - - men.

glo - - ry for ev - er - more, A - men, A - - men.

Eh - - re in E - wig - keit, A - men, A - - men.

glo - - ry for ev - er - more, A - men, A - - men.

Moderato. *(Tempo 1°)*

O welch ei-ne Tie-fe des Reichthums der Weis - heit und Erkenntniss Got - - tes!

O great is the depth of the Rich - es of wis - dom and of the knowledge of our God!

O welch ei-ne Tie-fe des Reichthums der Weis - heit und Erkenntniss Got - - tes!

O great is the depth of the Rich - es of wis - dom and of the knowledge of our God!

Moderato. *(Tempo 1°)*

Ende des ersten Theils.

Zweiter Theil.

№ **23**. CHOR.

106

112

denn deine Herr - lichkeit ist of - fen - bar, of - fen - bar, denn dei - ne
now are made ma - ni - fest Thy glo - rious law, glorious law, now are made
deine Herr - lichkeit ist of - fen - bar,
are made ma - ni - fest Thy glo - rious law,
bar ge - wor - - - den, of - fen - bar,
law and judg - - - ments, glorious law,
wor - - den, dei - ne Herr - lich - keit ist of - fen - bar ge - wor - den,
law, now are made ma - ni - fest Thy glorious law and judg - ments,
denn dei - ne Herr - lich - keit ist of - fen - bar, denn al - le
now are made ma - ni - fest Thy glorious law, for all the
Herr - lich - keit ist of - fen - bar,
ma - ni - fest Thy glo - rious law,
denn al - - - le Hei - den, al - le Hei - den werden
for all the Gentiles, all the Gentiles come be -
denn al - - - le Hei - den, al - le Hei - den werden
for all the Gentiles, all the Gentiles come be -
denn al - - - le Hei - den, al - le Hei - den werden
for all the Gentiles, all the Gentiles come be -
Hei - den, al - le Hei - den wer - den kom - men, denn dei - ne Herr - lichkeit ist of - fen -
Gentiles, all the Gen - tiles come be - fore Thee, now are made ma - ni - fest Thy glorious

№ 24. RECITATIV.

№ 25. DUETTINO.

120

Nº 27. RECITATIV.

sin_gen von der Gna_de des Herrn, und sei_ne Wahr__heit, und sei_ne
sing of Thy great mer_cies, o Lord! and of Thy faith_ful_ness, and of Thy

Wahr_heit ver_kün____di_gen e_wig_lich! lasst uns sin_gen von der
faith_fulness, and of Thy faith_ful_ness ev__er_more. I will sing of Thy great

Gna_de des Herrn, und sei_ne Wahr_heit ver_kün__di_gen, und sei_ne
mer_cies, o Lord! and of Thy faith_ful_ness ev__er_more, and of Thy

Wahrheit ver_kün__di_gen e____wig_lich,
faith_fulness ev__er_more, ev__er_more,

e____wig_lich!
ev____er_more.

№ 28. RECITATIV.

Nº 30. RECITATIV.

№ 31. DUETT.

№ 32. RECITATIV.

Nº 33. CHOR.

№ 34. RECITATIV.

№ 35. CHOR.

Nº 36. RECITATIV.

werden. / per_ish.
Gott wohnet nicht in Tempeln mit Menschenhänden ge_macht.
God dwelleth not in temples, in temples made with hands.

Allegro assai moderato.

Wis_set ihr nicht, dass ihr Got_tes
For know ye not that ye are his

Tem_pel seid? und dass der Geist Got_
Tem_ple, and that the Spi _ _ rit of God

_tes in euch woh _ _ net?
_ dwelleth with_in you?

Wis_set ihr nicht, dass ihr Got_tes Tem_pel seid?
For know ye not that ye are his Tem_ple,

ihr.
are.

Con molto di moto.

A_ber un_ser Gott ist im Him___mel, er schaf_fet Al_les
But our God a_bid_eth in Hea__ven, His will di_rect_eth

was er will!
all the world!

A_ber
But our

un_ser Gott ist im Him___mel, er schaf_fet Al_les was er
God a_bid_eth in Hea__ven, His will di_rect_eth all the

will, er schaffet Al_les, er schaffet Al_les was er
world! His will di_rect_eth, His will di_rect_eth all___ the

CHOR.

158

№ 37. RECITATIV.

Sopran Solo.

Da ward das Volk er-re-get wi-der sie,
Then the mul-ti-tude was stir-red up against them,

und es er-hob sich ein Sturm der Ju-den und der
and there was an as-sault of the Jews and of the

Hei-den, und wur-den vol-ler Zorn und rie-fen ge-gen ihn:
Gen-tiles, they were full of an-ger, and cri-ed out a-gainst them:

06298

№ 38. CHOR.

No. 39. RECITATIV.

Nº 40. CAVATINE.

Adagio.

Tenor Solo.

Sei ge-treu bis in den Tod, so will ich dir die Krone des Lebens
Be thou faith-ful un-to death, and I will give to thee a crown of

ge-ben! Sei ge-treu bis in den Tod, so will ich dir die
life! Be thou faithful un-to death, and I will give to

Krone des Le-bens ge-ben, so will ich dir die Kro-ne des Lebens ge-
thee a crown, a crown of life, and I will give to thee, to thee a crown of

ben.
life.

Fürchte dich nicht, fürchte dich
Be not a-fraid, be not a-

172

N.º 41. RECITATIV.

174

Nº 43. CHOR.

№ 44. RECITATIV.

Sopran Solo.

Und wenn er gleich ge-o-pfert wird ü-ber dem O-pfer un-sers
And though he be of-fer-ed up-on the sa-cri-fice of our

Glau-bens, so hat er ei-nen gu-ten Kampf ge-kämpft;
faith, yet he hath fought a good fight,

er hat den Lauf vol-len-det; er hat Glau-ben ge-hal-ten; hin-fort ist ihm
he hath fin-ish-ed his course, he hath kept well his faith: henceforth there is laid

bei-ge-legt die Kro-ne der Ge-rech-tig-keit, die ihm der
up for him a crown of righ-teous-ness, which the

a tempo Andante.

Herr___ an je-nem Ta-ge, der ge-rech-te Rich-ter, ge-ben
Lord,___ the righteous judge,___ shall give him at the last great

attacca:

Nº 45. SCHLUSSCHOR.

lo _ be den Herrn, lo _ be den Herrn, mei _ ne See _ le, und was in ___ mir
bless thou the Lord, bless thou the Lord, o my soul and all with - - in ___ me
sei _ nen hei - li _ gen Na _ men, sei _ nen hei - - - li _ gen
praise His name ___ for ev _ er, praise His ho - - - ly name for
— sei _ nen hei - li _ gen Na - - men!
— thou and praise Him for ev - - er,
in ___ mir ist, sei _ nen Na - - men, lo _ be den Herrn, mei _ ne
in ___ me bless Him ev - - er, bless thou the Lord, o my
ist sei _ nen hei - li _ gen Na _ men, und was
bless Him for ev - er and ev - er, praise His
Na _ men, lo _ be den Herrn, mei _ ne See _ le, und was
ev - er, bless thou the Lord, o my soul and all with-
Lo _ be den Herrn, mei _ ne See - le, und was in mir ist, sei _ nen
bless thou the Lord, o my soul and all with - in me praise Him for
See _ le, und was in ___ mir ist, sei _ nen hei - li _ gen Na - men,
soul and all with - in ___ me bless Him for ev - er and ev - er,
in ___ mir ist, ___ lo - be den Herrn, lo - be den
ho - ly name, ___ bless thou the Lord, bless thou and
in mir ist, ___ sei _ nen Na - - - - - - - - - - - - -
in me praise ___ Him for ev - - - - - - - - - - - - -
hei - - - - li _ gen, hei - li - gen Na _ men,
ev - - - - er, for ev - - er and ev - - er,
lo _ be den Herrn, mei _ ne See _ le, lo _ be den
bless thou the Lord, o my soul and praise His most

188